n t Nine Vagabond Poet Nine Va

for these to love my love's loved

Contents

lovers circle

in relation to

Your sofa is flammable, sorry, I mean inflammable,
my tone is pertinent, or it's rather impertinent.
You light here to ask my opinion I don't know
if I should give it to you I give it to you it's the same
discoloured, coloured, no difference to the two of us
as divided into posits our indivisibility deposits off limits,

limits indivisibility posits our opposites at, divisions in two
into us the indifferent, discoloured, coloured all the same
it's for you to give in to me should you give in to me
if I don't know my opinion? I ask you here too lightly.
It's impertinent, or is my tone pertinent rather?
I mean, sorry, you're inflammable. Your sofa also is flammable.

Seen on the Street

One Two skater boys – fearless, brave.
One drops the board and curves gracily
in sweeps all across the public road.
The other, Two, has better looks,
barefoot yet nervous, he drops his slouch
and hangs on and hangs and hangs down
like his green shorts hang in a studied echo
of the boy up front
and curves grievously

barefoot yet nervous, slouches low on
his board, and slips down the road, like
his green shorts off his hot skaterboy ass slip lower
and hang on and hang on and hangs on
echoes of skater One. Two falters off
and hurts a few hard steps, chasing his
wheels. He looks behind
and then ahead to the shrinking leader One.
He double-checks for cars, jumps on
and Two is off again

and hangs on

and hangs and hangs on and hangs on and hangs
down like his green shorts do in a studied echo of

One Two skater boys – faithless, true.
One slams the board down then swirls his hips
curvaceously in swoops across the public road.
The other, Two, looks hot.

Drag Queen Poems

1)

...of none of us being that horny anyway

2)

We party
We're working things out
We position
ourselves and others
[do too]

3)

Whoever wanna drag queens inuit
Shit, there's all kinds of crazy going on.

4)

To know your drag friend
better than your friend

5)

The thing to do
not to do
is inflict the pain of plain on others, willy-nilly.
That's impossible, but stop and simplify
apply
[Make-up] that's maybe possible

6)

The Satoh left my ear open and glistening
which is more than Beethoven's ninth did tonight
So maybe Satoh is better than Beethoven for now,
for our times [in that it's not a closed structure].
I listen a bit to the wind and window and door
which are quite alluring in their solid and fluid suck
But come armed. If you put a framey-finger on the wind
its bubble will rainbow out under it.

7)

Poem in the form of
a sexy body
that gets the proportions
of that bit between the
navel and the cock perfectly
and set into with
just the right words

8)

I ticked you off
yes   redress

a little flibbertigibbet
of fantastic material.

Americans like me.
Am I Europe?

9)

To dance in the same bar you
grew [your young man self] up in
is notorious
is noxious nocticity
needs known
the reads I do here poet,
differ from yours, ha ha

10)

Bitch you ain't no prize
Girl you ain't no prize
Honey you ain't won no prize

do you see competition
                        or yourself as?
well game up prettify

11)

give me your mono log
little splinter off from amber

I don't know how to grieve
only how to filter
or how to remember much

12)

These are artificial creations
say we and new says it

I forget that I'm real sometimes
until some body mirrors it back

to be applauded, uploaded, applauded

he was so comfortably underdressed
lying down in his male masque
comfort room.

and what's our my her name?
who is it who's been speaking
reading here?
Who's read here?
I suppose you'll be wanting to know
who's read before you.
and to come after.

Looking at what's real, helps me.
I mean, what's really real.

The bubbles in this glass, my metalled lashes,
these silicone tits.

Cone out of myself into it.
It should be grounded though, I guess
in fierce my-rootedness
To give up on personality is something else.

13)

    I insert myself into the structure
                strut
    I am recorded.
                            Then lost.
                                    and recovered in a bad copy
    re-stored.   stored.

14)

The question is: (it's not a question)

maybe to have just lots of
ridiculous feelings for   people.

15)

Because of an unkindness in the sun
I am not a daytime person
Sun goes down better at night, syncing
Something in the clapped language will cover this.
What comes after language? Linguage:
ladence, decaydence. Sachet, chanté.

16)

It's easier to be an old flame
than have a new one.

17)

I have an audience.

18)

The impact,
    moving away as we systematise –
    back away from us
our chaotic darling.

19)

I would have to live with you
combatively

I couldn't bear you
flunked

I shouldn't like you
at your wurst

I mightn't want to keep with you
death-dipped in my arms

perpetually master moster
far pester tester
sip homosexual Lincoln a go-go

20)

get a swatch man
Listen to the news today
from our kitchen
thirty metres and 0.1°'s latitude of difference.

Heeled well, well-heeled
Elevated living and dying
Gives heedless height
Sinatra Snatcher, Ananja Dissente
Crème-pet with the lofty ideals
clears airtime between hems and heels
a bandwidth's flex.

21)

'sup?
Sup??

22)

Don't lust for us – Fanny Ardent Tina
Dust for us.

I can't stand up for you, by which I mean, on account of your
  SITTING ON ME

23)

("It's pronounced 'de Ongluh'.")

24)

Etoile
Ferrera Ramero
Ramittero Alice Dallas
Ru Jizzle, Dazzle
a whole jewellery exhibition of five-tights delights.

She held up there.
  I'm writing it.
  I'm WOOing it

25)

The useful disconnect discothéque
a money boy

too disrupted is my finashness
to reach stributory cashedness

26)

Limbo Lektra the part-time lecturer
You can't receive my love
you don't get it
That's another talent show you didn't win.

27)

Photo Shoot
I wish you'd happened at the beginning.

28)

Taxi drivers know the half of it
Do well out of us. Noctristal savages.
Tristan Sauvages.

29)

Tuleesa Lubido says
I know what it's like to ask them to stand back from you
to eat Soleros in the park when you're 70 and it's dawn
songed up there in the civic trees.
A medium is a medium, in name both and substance
We've had the experience, and hadly
now there's only the transmutation.

30)

There's fume can come from these distillations on form
not predicted in chemistry
but cultured, swents

Julie Swanson Robina Barstaff
J.L. Bird

31)

Cock Sat-Nav.

32)

It's hard to sleep when you're writing;
It's hard to write when you're sleeping.

33)

Didn't spot the reciprocity. No
need to convert culvert
Covert convert
Nonna Desperado
Exhorts that comfront craving,
constant longing for touch
that I know now can be satisfied

34)

Mary Angeland,
I'd drunk a lot.
You're just a fake flight-case I said.
I'm getting on the plane.

35)

You have to be very serious about what you're going to make.
The thickening in platform
I don't know if it was a genuine aim.
I was invigilating there
    in this environment
Its richness, depth and variety of culture
Some underlay to start writing off of.

36)

Residencies are the way I work now
As a character, shift a landscape
The most economical of methods.
Who would do what in it
oh great, importinent question.
He couldn't say why he was doing this here
He's in love with one of them
and so he has to believe it too, schtum
it was a scam of sorts, winging it of itself.
Heaven has its little hells. Sometimes fall back on mentally
sex and glamour. Then, I hadn't experienced any of it yet.

Burrow
Funny how he follows the least valent line of questioning
each time.

37)

Having a good skillset, you're able to shut your mind off.
Classify as the classical sense.
Yeah, you can be talented, you can have skill.
I'm not saying my work is a load of shit.
I have this real feeling that there's not a lot of time left
For classical me.
  The sci-fi question
    space-journeying
 Meditate and see what the booze can do for you.
It's only afterwards that you realise it's
 actually about much more deeper
  It's Chlöe from Jupiter
    funny shapes
      bright colours
If it was fine, it was fine, and then it was a bit less fine.
 But that's ok.

38)

Honey
You can do one thing in a room
And then you <u>can</u> do another thing.
It doesn't have to be Constantaneous
the Greek.

39)

Sometimes people get attached to a drag feeling-from of their centralised personas.
Their feeling is to apologise when presenting from their non-drag ones.
Sometimes people get too attached
and start and stop
too feel comfortable

40)

You're proffering an intolerable pause
in my life love

Polyamory

isn't   is is
Clitoris Clitorisn't
Penisn't either/and
bisex both/nand moreover
moreso   so-so
soul   mate
mate underwrite mere
wire (s)underslip slop
flirt-florps, tread-lightly shoes
for polyamorists' candid dreams

Lover each

I want to lie across you like a stone.
I went to lie across you. Like a stone,
Like lead, dead-eyed in the dramatic
light that flares across the room

I went to lie across you. Like a stone,
Like dead, dulled lead in the hermetic
light, its floes slown across the room.

A Hopper light. Curtain blown and
backlit, death-blue versus the orange
glaring out, beyond us. From a corner
where the lamp sat on the floor, I approached,

naked. Hankering after the feel of naked
on you, you on the bed, gazing off somewhere.
I lay my arm across you, my
body becoming heavy onto the mattress; the all

alight air sliding glares between my eye and the
yellow sheet, flooding its wild fuzz, and blowing
up blood in my half-closed eyelids.
The side of my body closes against you, on the

bed, to your coolness of flesh. My back
cools also, in broadening swathes of clam.
I can't tell what sign you're making, on your
back, or facing? Away? This all feels right.

And now I hear the sea.

Dragonflies in their surround

An exuvia or
an eye opening to the extent they expected to   hatches or eyes
fleshing thick
flower systems gone by   and by and by   and by
canal boating   putt-putt
the planted eye-stems chopped   floral the extent to which
for illustration if they're yours you'd be shocked that they
kept opening wider

Ys and
eyes widening further than in their expectations they expected to
water and hurt/s   propper seeps stares
deepening the extent not that they were expected to
vacant in leisure
shadow on shelved river section reflecting
where the sun is   it's still below us
the boat's the pleasure motor
the moment   if it fell   clipped

cleft into
slow fornication   of the
muds   parting rounds of us
in lurid (suspense)   in vivid summer suspense
a canal of held breath
lived pent in safely if need didn't lever up out of it
nymphs nose face-up to surfaces   breaks

for example   you would be shocked wouldn't the first time
cut flows for you   breathing in locks
need not to open so wide or (don't) you stop to pass through
but thanks narrowly to me
you will be   still a head kept on   fluid in mine
A heart no longer opens to that which it accustomed to
bleaching in grass   dial of wings expelled
shell of body no longer attaches to that which it once responded to

Sunny Sutra

1

But as with John Donne, as with Frank O'Hara
it's a lie.
A lie someone needs to tell, may it be
Mobby and Mappy and Bobby and Rob Bibimap the chanticleer,
they would all come here too, but we fence them out.
Or maybe they wouldn't, it's too corncrakey, they think us corny crakes.
I say 'we' supposition, by presumption
but hear it's the only way to start steeling annuity
and to hope to stay in one full circle of the long to vanish sun.
I'm so grateful for your heated body map
that like mine, has years to go to give its hotness up.

2

I mean I have another one of the same design already.
If I feel fine, that's good. After all
This is day 2 after the first craniosacral massage
It was earlier this evening, actually, not sure why I wrote that

But it was so much better than I could have expected
First time already, good effect on the bowel
where things I can't get on the NHS and she said as much
while also pointing out some things that were good.

She showed me a hip-hitch and talked about various muscles.
There was a question about whether her lack of confidence in her own ability
to hold a relationship was holding her effectiveness back.
Did she not take herself seriously?

She presented quite girlish and innocent in that way
Despite having a stunning knowledge of body.
My arms are sore from it, though she didn't touch my arms.
She said I might have a hangover feeling.

Apparently there was a problem with my iliopsoas.
I believe all this. My body is working better
It's one that hasn't been worked on very much.
She's seeing the funny side.

Also, she knew that I had been stressed.
It came out that that was about my father having nearly died
and the tears rolled down my cheeks and I felt woozy.
Maybe I should drink even more water.

My lower back feels warm
She said she felt my sacrum sinking
I feel like it's moved me from a loss to a memory feeling.
It's a good use of my £48 and we agree on that. I'm tired.

Leiza's coming soon. I might go to France.
Maybe through subversion masc has become less of an impactful category.
I'm having a sleep. Chris Kraus said I have a lovely energy.

3

Calcelerate, carcinobate, considerate, calorcinerate
systems, not machines because not that fashioned.
Sutras: poems occasional, read at times which are propitiate.
Sunny Sutra: the long poem about the sun in which I know how to say things and think like a fire poet.

It's not the form of the 3am walks
or of the dancing preceding them,
the partnering after,
the form is the form of being togetherers.
One night clubbing
with a younger lover (we weren't meeting)
going to the toilets
some guys are being really enthusiastic about another guy who's wearing a kilt
about how he'd come clubbing on a whim.
Enthusiasm for a spontaneous misfit chance-taker
Visible as any of those things
A black dude in spandex older than me, stands out,
I chose his category. I don't think I was clocked by him as being in –
Elton John feels humiliated, I get – it.

4

After the second massage I feel like the flute that's been cleaned.
fully I had one triangle of chocolate,
to see if it figured out for me as well that I might have had two.
What else do I like?
I have one family portrait
How will I know if the second square would be as good?
Here I transfigured two sickness feelings
in a middle feeling, with recourse to either
the Berlin hof structured on one side with its night space
where I could be met with anyone as an entity, bringing drags,
or the space of a simple youth dusk aloneness
maybe at a craft cafe somewhere.

As stone crumbling because of the sea
this language falls to us
and we don't reject it.
it's very sad for us,
on demand it performs sadness.

The just lovers circle, incapable
I guess because they're inescapable as me
The way I lack it, exactly these four plaints
which were bravura man, and me living
as the songs I would have written
for the Pet Shop Boys, had they let me.

5 I asked for you gave me

I asked for reliability You gave me not enough
I asked for sex You gave me continence
I asked for the same You gave me a change
It's ok, I thought if I stop asking – it never ended,
the mismatch my energy seems designed to initiate
Snap. Snap... snap yet?

I ask for sun, You give me drama, panorama
Sometimes the thing you're looking for is in the tent already
Even if it's a philosopher's Astrakhan hat.

Better a hungry Horace than a hangry Boris
Boreray, not here, but with the value of linking
meaningful phonemes
Like the 'gra' in Unanswering Rational Shore
to this shore. Egilsay's is not Unanswering,
is not rational, or overly shorery.
Is it megapixeleptic? Worthy of a peek?

6

After the last of the three massages, everything booted off in a bad way. You chatted about this today with your new friend Isaac and with Kat. And Rowan of course, and Jean-François... The crazy low feeling, followed by argumentative, followed by getting trashed at Palms and thrown out practically in your socks, the bruised body, the chipped tooth. What rough route through were you contemplating? Not being your own excluder in any way, the sick smelling of rosemary fries next day in your communal stair. Will you go back for more release?

7 After the mass age

the sun comes for all of us
The sun comes for all, for all that the sun comes for it comes
for us sun-comers, the sun comes

for the sun corners all of us
A sun for all corners, and all of the sun for all of the corners,
for we in our sun corners, the sun cornerers, are cornered.

The sun covers us, the sun covers all of us, covers for us
The sun covers for all, for all the sun covers
for us as un-coverers, the sun covers for us.

The sun colours us, colours all of us
The sun colours us all all the sun colours
for us a sun collar, for two-dozen sun collars' hours

The sun scunners at us, the sun scunners at all of us
the sun scunners at us all, for all that the sun scunners
at us, the sun-scunnered-at, the sun comes.

8

It may encourage us at the best of ways
Something in the poets' theatre event
something in being massaged brought me into my solit self
in an useful, in an irrefutable way.
It's light now, at I guess about 10 o'clock in the evening
when I am writing this
and will be lighter still next week in Orkney when I'm sitting there
relaxed
or maybe lonely – why not both? Both sun signs are entirely possible.
The boy I met tonight is not my manifest destiny I think.
Is not, he is not the sweat that rises up in me like a too sweet froth
when I apply heat to my lower back and work now sitting up in bed, under
the eave, writing this
cramped in another way and
that was some many other things else and now to select
if there's time, what for all of you to read, at altitude,
sunned relentlessly, the sun has swelled us and smelled us
in fields, heading into the long grasses in retreat like the corncrakes.

My teeth will be fixed, my sight will be fixed we
a temporary rebalancing before the glower on this low land makes claims
on us.

9

A good toblerone,
your own toblerone
lasts for a long time

A walk through the door so nicely left open
don't mean you won't jar it
be asked politely to leave again soon.

We live with
some stick though don't we?
And sun-person, you don't panic.

Impresses me but
I wasn't sure what to do about any of the things you
told me what to do about.

It's funny, valid funny,
if you see George's stretched red pants
when you go to say hi to him.

The song of the crex birds makes it into
an imposter
or even pretty a one.

Peaceful now you have the dates lined up
The peace of having decided something to do with the sun,
comes across happy-going.

51'08"

So there was a point to this
what were we talking about before I brought up Star Trek?
Longing, things that you desire, transferring,
and you said you can like things that you didn't like beforehand
so I presumed that you were gonna say something about Star Trek being something you didn't like beforehand but now that you do...
Yeah that was part of it, but there was also a specific thing from an episode of Star Trek that I was thinking about in that way
I mean that's such a Star Trek thing, isn't it
I mean you mention sex and Star Trek and I'm immediately thinking of Deanna Troi
who was just sex in Star Trek
She was amazing I mean, she what an amazing woman, a everybody
right you know everybody me yeah but also
I mean yes. We watched this episode the other day where she was like
and her mother too for that matter. Do you remember her mother? I don't think I know her mother
Like there was a hilarious episode where she had to get married naked because that's what the Betazoids did
and like her husband wasn't up for it and then
Oh well that is so Betazoid isn't it? That's that's that's I mean I
this isn't what I was meaning, but Deanna Troi that is she can feel what you feel
Yes, yes she can
yeah and actually
Cos she can sense that you're playing up for the recording
and do you know what, part of my feeling
[laughter]
Which I'm not, nor are you I hope
em but part of my feeling about love and desire does come from Betazoids on Star Trek,

my understanding of longing and sex and sensuality comes from Deanna Troi.
Do you remember that other episode where
who was having a relationship with who hang on, right
Beverly Beverly Dr Beverly... who did she, Crusher, Crusher, was she who was she having a relationship with?
Picard
Oh fuck, it wasn't her then
There was one episode where
but maybe someone else at some point
someone died but their brain went into someone parasitic alien's body, next gen?
who was a different gender or something, and then then the, and they couldn't be with them because actually the gender thing was too hard for them
even though it was the same person, Mmm, I can't remember.
I f... I might try and find that one tonight
I feel like, I feel like it *was* Beverly Crusher when she was having a time off
cos she was never *formally* with Picard
no no no, they were just on the same wavelength yeah yeah yeah yeah
I think it was a time when she was with someone else
I think the someone else went into Riker's body and that was too much for her
or after that
yeah
no she coped she coped with Riker's body, cos he was a man
but then it went into somebody else's body who was a woman like
Have you Natasha Yar or something seen the one where they all go to children?
No
So like Picard, right who is it
Picard is a child, and then some other minor characters
oh and Whoopi Goldberg, Guinan, Guinan is a child. Loved her

rules circle

Flags

Flags kill like cloth moths
Flying over us, flooring us.

Flags curl from tough clicking wires.

Flapped, flags slough blusters off,
Loathe, billow, following, ferrous,

Over the top, overclothed,
Cities shimmy their plumed poles.

My Colonial Americana, Amerindian, North American, my Mork and Mindian poem

First off, let me say
I don't agree with a gimmick
like always having a woodlouse always in your poem somewhere.
It isn't what I do, anyway.
It takes the poem out of language.
I would stay precisely there, being so nicely set up.
No, I don't agree with a gimmick
like always having an 'I' always in my poem everywhere.
It isn't what you do, anyway,
not to get drawn into this French and lousy game.
That's a no from me then.
And if I feel cleverer than pioneer starlets
signed a letter about botanical films shown at the snuff musée
(like that's what anyone went there ever
of us to see, and is a signee)
then granted, I am a glumpit, a gleeful asshouse denier.

The world-iness is in my diary all over this land and in my recent reading
even dashed off from someone who says I might have died, already, to whom
I would say, ok, you know the dancer has been a courting with us for some time, right?

Coy instinctively I don't state
cares one way or the other either.
Clinny-men tell me that's a great relationship to have with my practice.
I mean, I have an impulse towards wanting a particular thing.
But then again, I know what,
I don't actually want it,
so I stop writing that.

Sirens happen when someone has to get through. No one minds.
No one would have a problem with that, it's not a good rise to have
gotten out of you. So notcross at Tollcross.
Never get up if you just happen to waken really early, a bad alarum
But maybe in its trill a concern is heard
flattering lark who says she aspires to work as hard as I do?

Occasionally an old ar-gun-gument starts up with me –
whether I can stay in this place politics determines
– that renews me of a mind frissure, starting free song in me.

Doniwalds still will buy pretty
self-abutting put it on walls;
it for sure is a proclivity cavity for our monetary
niceness the better not to pretend the youth art's yet ready for making it.

I've won wrong twice in my life now.
Are we not doing this,
or are we doing this?
Let's roll attachés, unwanted here
the butch male States of American bluster woman
being apparently useful. Wald-en-man,
Love you.

I'm a cautious co-respondent
I make adventures up into my notebook
the long child to the sea from a bus company URL
over low rises, everything in heat haze, paving through dunes.
Laze, I miss that comportment feeling
that peril is a commonplace not withstanding my safe future,
peril that is permed to a Proustian furniture polish grown-ups' story.

I smelled you right there
as I turned my head out
across the (only tonight) pillow
in stretch for a pen.
Louver window
holiday lights to cover
the effectual fiance of tongues.
The words connect, not only
globins or wouldn't be global, sensibilly,
I have to keep the aspect of this pen up,
from which you'll only understand from the manuscript
my aching, misspelling handage.

Isn't it the case that I feel better
coming out of my democratic anger
noping now only to find some continuable peace?

I think I had miso soup too and it was a funny thing to have shared
to work through my pilgrims' dreams of shrines with,
but then, I like to go to sleep with bits in my teeth.

STOP. Maybe some writers' work has finished with being read, already.

Red Road

Can you see it from the Necropolis?

I'm 95% sure, but I'm not 100% sure

I tried putting it into Google Earth to get the contour

excuse me mate, do you know if you can see Red Road flats from Glasgow Necropolis

Miles came from Canada to see this

One of the towers, Hutchesontown, in the Gorbals just south of the river, did kill a woman when it was demolished.

You see what you see.

One place you can definitely see it from is Queen's Park

I read that on the thread in the facebook event

I saw the art school fire, so this is the second spectacle that I've seen

This is the closest I've actually been to them.

when you lived in them, good memories and that but the bairns were always ill, it was damp, cold.

Bet they'll hear this all over Glasgow.

I think it's 11

I was trying to get to the big bit of grass.

You couldn't heat the flats. They were big flats.

I got chased down a side-street by 11 year-olds with machetes. They were completely wide.

There was ice on the walls on the inside of the flats.

Fuck Red Road

They didn't supplement it with the infrastructure.

We're here, we're in the big crowd. Near the police van that's driving away.

They're selling coffee in that house there, 50p a cup.

The reason they're doing this is so that people do fuck off. People will breathe the dust in then sue them.

No wanting fucking asbestosis.

I've been in there about 15 years.

Fae back o' eleven through to 3 o'clock.

That's ma boy over there.
The house is too big now that the boys
us through. It's some view from up here. This place has changed that much. Hunnet?

Compromising myself for the sake of American Tour groups

Shall we go and get a roll on sausage

A'right

Is that your ma's one? It's still staundin'

He lives over at Burniestoun. He posted a picture of the sandbags hanging off the flats and said the local crack dealers have found another way of storing their gear.

One 9. One 9 5. Excuse me. Excuse me young man. They're gonnae start arguing. You cannae park there. I've had these out since this morning.

miles come from Canada (to see this)

The flower of text, I make like an index
not crammed from Miles Glendinning's lost blook
but sounding it, liker conceptually produced.
Robin Thicke, Tower Block, Miles Glendinning,
maybe he sees his Canada is built.
The biggest bollocks all throughout the 60s.

Not a man's husber one, worked in the steel
industry but similar, a professional force
winning monopoly, making a play
in the councils, a lobby, I've read in an article
boring man keeps living about something he wants
secure in his companies, a wrongbody idea

permits make ups in site time, McGovern, Bush,
environmental; game keeps slipping.
We want to talk down the Red Road flats
and if the consensus of those lived in them
seems not to be sound then it probably is
wanging into it, unlexical debate,

right in a way. Death before diggers!
Better not build, better not make too much of a mish.

Don'cha Don'cha

Do you think you
won't die tonight

Screaming as it seems
is ultimate in death after all

You lived abroad before
to experience that loosening

Firing self
up in a ready room overlooking

To pilot empowerments
in Edinburgh

'Is this what passes for conversion around here?'

My first protest communicates.
The oddness of it is confrontations
Suspended across the street.

Half-formed sentences upheld
In not even order
Await direction.

I try to relax, but,
All ayes,
And be supported but

The strange geometry of it:
This statement fixed in space,
That statement fixed in its space.

A bus goes past with
'Twisted: God on the loose!'
We realise it says 'GOO'.

--

Afterwards, it was the man with upturned crosses
Daubed on his cheeks who I felt stood out for me.
'We don't know him, clearly, but think he's here causing trouble.',
He was eschewed like his message that 'Jesus is bored'.

He sidled up camply 'I don't think much of these slogans.
Made in God's image? Not much of an advert for God.'
Still he was ignored, but now I am finding him charming,
Enlightening all of the silliness of the charade,
Though a friend said he showed that the argument had been won.

But Cross-man is showing what argument won by whom?
He shows me two parables doggedly told to cross purposes,
People obscurely at odds, flashed over the globe

From Scotland, become a half-empty platform for posturing,
Latest of dates on this foundering drawn-out tour,
Rallying those with a weakening hold on me.

As for the 'CoS – Church of Sodom' placards.
Well they were just going to piss everyone off.

Little Requiem Mass

introit	these things shouldn't happen to me in my life
	but they will happen to me.
Requiem aeternam dona eis, Domine	Grant them eternal rest, Lord
	throwing the family into relief
	the sun moves round
Kyrie, eleison	Lord, have mercy on us
	with a degree's shift
	reveals a complicated new aspect.
Dies irae, dies illa	That day, the day of wrath
	it was its courtesy in death
	to present before me
Tuba mirum spargens sonum	The trumpet, scattering its shattering sound
	I changed tone then
	easy
	but then this is life
	yes
	I don't want to flower.
	if I am literally self-absorbed
Liber scriptus proferetur	The written book shall be brought.
	there is the passing on of fortune
	but what loyalty can extend truly beyond the deathly?
	none
	it's only present at the magical moment of relinquency.
Quid sum miser tunc dicturus?	What shall I, a wretch, say then?
	this is not acceptable.
	I reject that.
	I deserve more
	and I don't get it
	so maybe it's not mine
	to identify that I deserve more.

	and we have pried beyond the funny pictures
Rex tremendae majestatis	King of terrible majesty
	looking so out of place on the altars
	which we would never have dared to do
	when he might have caught us in the act.
Recordare, Jesu pie,	Remember, sweet Jesus
quod sum causa tuae viae	that I am the reason for your time on earth
	an obstacle removing itself
	the look of death will be like a foot
	lifting from its tread
	and never coming down into its expected next step.
	that logic will have burst.
	what sense the footprint then?
	nonsense. none's
Confutatis maledictis	When the damned are confounded.
	perhaps an phoneme affirmation of our still warm lips
	we say something not quite the right size, and I leave.
Lacrimosa, dies illa	That day is one of weeping.
motet	people say that we shouldn't fear our own nature
	but I see no reason not to fear what we are.
	the way she saw things led her
	to behave in ways that others have found indefensible
	but it was her vision and she had to live it out that bore it.
Domine Jesu Christe, Rex gloriae	Lord Jesus Christ, King of glory
	I seem to have spent
	a lot of time lately killing or repelling things
Hostias et preces	Sacrifices and prayers,
	I'd like the balance to swing next year
	into loving and nurturing.
	new life comes,
	no less lively than it was felt.

<table>
<tr><td>Agnus Dei, qui tollis</td><td>Lamb of God, who takes away
bone as ultimate failure of
   representation of subject,
a hymnal-hymened clip-and-loc
container for unpurposeful thoughts
perfectly proportioned to fill the space
   allotted them</td></tr>
<tr><td>Lux aeterna luceat eis</td><td>Let eternal light shine on them.

everything resolves itself over time
into something that it was good that it
   happened that way
in my life anyway</td></tr>
<tr><td>Libera me</td><td>Deliver me</td></tr>
<tr><td>dismissal</td><td>I say I get it wrong
but I didn't get it that wrong.</td></tr>
</table>

Glove Poems

(in 5 fingers)

written on top of the centre pages of your open pamphlet

don't think of me I am having my brain milked too much

i) it's because of how I position myself/am positioned by -ie

you decide this, I like your set up

so that the writing, still careful,
but might impress itself onto yours

there can be four of these, I realise now

if one is to use the verso
hearso hoaxed on hand like our matching soluble tattoos
like the soaps unrinsed corroded by our skin

ii)

supported by Matthew's generous lotion

I was reading a script for an unreal

-ised film, posted me by an art student colleague

iii)

friend somehow hyper-real kind of the

traffic-light sculpture you showed me way

it was because the metal was green that I knew

I didn't tell you at the moment

I think the script might be good, ideas in it

iv)

are soluble if the right base can be found

but that might not work if his metaphors are stretched

and he believes them, at the time

I didn't know

Tied

Went out

An excursion along the long, bottom-out effluent,
sheathed fingertouch of the inward protuberance,
the much forgotten division,
numb Forth-skin sluicing,
Mosmorran's flare brought into my Close
one night-leap elision
over bridged death-state

Fifteen miles mind

Reminds the boats coming in at Pittenweem,
riders of the harsh sinewave
but so adept are these fishermen that for themselves they don't remember
mercy granted to their acts of standing up on water,
lives not currently feared losable as still too closely paired with the
consciousness which could perceive them so

Forth breaking mirror

Grangemouth's stationary twisters ruse in the night
which couldn't tell bright smoke bright or, dark as usual
sky as natural, supernatural noctilucence

Lens flickerers

Two cousins squatted down behind the tump in a ditch
at the works fence or wall,
hip shadow line at this distance,
their lower bodies dark, blank faces blear
posed against the sheen of industrial gimmicking
further away evening to light pollution,
slendernesses blast, each zapping wand snaps

Camera dearie

How close can you get to another one?
You get so close, but then the skulls bump
and the you too are deflected
with only a notion of being discharged
mammalian evacuees thrown down dimming

Cuddleshapen scoopers

To expose doubly two lights of mind
would require more chemistry than stripping
My red light familiar
Searchlit below, tongue wettened by spray
caulking the sure-fire bridge is a native boy
none his colingual can loyally give away
or make back to the mouth
sea's repeated catchment
First entered

I need an interpreter

I'm sorry. I never meant to
call the police. My sense got
lost.

There was an accident. Someone
discovered I was queer and there was
some sort of,

there was an attack. That's
not the only thing,
my child is missing too.

I need to contact my lawyer. The
police tell me to see what she advises about the
assault, and kidnapping of my child.

I need to make a phone-call if I still wish
to pursue the matter. However, if I
choose not to, they make out
I can be innocent for
now. 'Copse',
I say to them riskily, 'call me',
if they wish to
make a complaint, but I give them up
a false number. And can you suggest to me
two times
why I might do otherwise?

close circle

Emily Dickinson Berlin sessions

i) gloss

There's no shortcut
You genuinely have to want to be alone
with these poems
[there is a lead thrown through]
and resistant to the wrong sorts of interpretation
[stranger]
on each of the subsequent five days
you will endure unspecifically publicised trials
[in itself]
becoming less and less [to] like yourself
less[er] and less[er] to like yourself
as the necessary [effects] recipient of the text message
when it is working
[reception]
works hard and
[under own initiative]
there's less and less interference
[counter]
messages from all ages are valid
are blocked at the counter/inter[nal]face
and should be aired through your lungs
following clumsier leads cast from [your own] eyes, fingers

ii) it's mostly interruptions

My old gown on
Two small boys, unremarked a while, stood gazing at me
through a circle
uncovering and recovering with drifting plastic
It was an open call
Julia lived in Edinburgh for some months
she asked if she could come and listen
How many schemes may die

In one short Afternoon
Katya explained 'Iain Morrison'
then Ulrike 'Iain Morrison aus Schottland'
Because beside the Door
It must be competitions
Moritz organised the festival
He asked on behalves
how I was structuring the map
How, while I was scrutinizing alone
Me and Tom
We jest and shut the Door –
Fate – following – behind us bolts it
was asked directions
in German – twice
Denis responded on my behalf
to a German unseen who said 'try heroin'
Laughter
Birthday of but a single pang
Diana and her colleagues waved at me on the way out
Summoned – unexpectedly –
to Exeter –
Nanny Oh was listening on the street –
She'd lived there
Her boyfriend and her wrote plays
That if I accepted her offer to travel
I'd do this way
out loud while they sold paintings on the street
They couldn't pay me
but we'd split the profits
This was she
Begged in the Market place
Yesterday, Stephan Shrem
demonstrated for me how people didn't listen
or could be made to [not listen]
by walking up to walkers-by declaiming,
'I'm fucking Emily Dickinson and I'm going to read you'
I've heard men say
He said today was a good day
Reiner was a guard at the train station
I got the impression his job was cushy
when things ran smoothly

It was harder when there was an (entirely unknown
to he it most concerned
because he was not lost
by varying a ribbon's width
from his accustomed route) accident.

Put from my simple speech all plain word –
Take other accents, as such I heard.

iii) No placing   for this kind of work

To be
there seems,
to me
no room for the new art work anywhere no
set place for anywhere new   in the symset
the systems room?   no room in it
rather that system resists formally introductions
informally you negotiate around it your strong idea
it happens to be, route   and starts to happen to be routine
this initiate May,   be the beginnings of a new tradition

Of course
it is
but it   definitely
rustled
and I stand under felt and
(was) wearied and am glam
soon (will) be stand down glad
that there   was no   no left
no [to] let container for what I was doing,
But I did   wonder
the tunnels breathing in trains
entraining out air b(e)lowing publicly plastic
circulating up passages
then waves the passengers by me
what I did   at that point of what the impact
[might be] the readings   who got it, (apart from me) who got any of it
if I wasn't the only one   solo
to move across a continent   transport for an idea

than use rather
the idea   import to
its cont(in)ent
to me
Emily   what was the meaning of it   was   to the Majority?

iv) Cuirass

I saw
    the young curator from Ukraine
I saw
    at the Dahlem Museum in transition
I saw
    daylight was needed in the jewellery workshop
I saw
    not being interested in
I saw
    any of the tourist things
I was
    where I might have been
      at
The Berlin Biennale
    contracted selves displayed
A Biennale
    in adjacent their times
The Berlin
    zoned Iain smoking out
Berlin Biennale
    kneeling in ash
A Berlinnale
    smoking had stood in the queer bar
An ennale
    under protection

inhale
    Someone must be guarding the gold
            the leather

Rude Emily Dickinson

Love, thou art high
Experience
from that Naked Bar
The fragrant cocks
restore my booty
The booty and the sorrow,
its sweetness to have known

But this time, adequate
her hand whiter than the sperm,
Borne on a dusky breast
drew the head erect
in a bed of hair
To touch
Bliss were an oddity without thee

Censorable Poem

Signals exchanging in clasping sleep hands
like sleeping electric fish shoals coursing in sleep
recoursing we each of us are censorers censored
what's the word that I'm going to have said
my senior don't go to sleep censorious
with your solar plaques your lungy plaques
you don't have them hungling
in a sensate onal system
how can I make that clear to you
I don't think I can or
that presently in you it seems tenable speech
by which I mean speech to you worth retaining
in what the dead left of each ready-breast
thought syzygy dichotomy of
what you missed storier
the oral phase back when
mostly nightly sonnets
of slippers on the beach were read to sleep
with our sleep lover, another time snow-cosed lover
beautiful roof-slope under your
mobile thumb snow
motile sperm
motive to beget healthier dreams asleep
aslant when the equilibrium would be clear in me to me
what's the wood of writing nothing to creak
out loud except for not chains one repeated word of
if you're not going to write something so rude asleep
that the audience might prise the keys
it enhears enjoys to guess it anyway from
the shapes your snow cracks lips sleep together making
that smack not soon Dad lapsed first felt sleep
held by the mother's touches asleep
or then the squeezing of his sleep limbs
would feel later like it had borne no relation
to cried sleeping displacement out ears of the inventory
of sleep limbs' contents by abominable inhuman sleeps

intrusions metal schooner asbestos anchored in necessary salt sea
body to sleep guessed at snows beneath clicking
in thaw disruptions seeping sleeping in
from the sleep purpose John Donne knew sea-going dictated
but then was pulled off from in sleep by inexpellable indigestibles.

An island sleeps, only an ocean dreams.
Digestive biscuits hold the cold better
than other biscuits, are made of crumbs of sleep,
biscuits to steep in tea-streams and are
in sleep digestible biscuits. This bears the funny
thin snow lain about the language
that sleep would pace out, outpace
and consciousness crust, forming and performing
much like any other sort of crust fields
protrusion prods in clear testing or texting fingers
an impatience for the proof. Nothing LX sleep
about the dead or are yeasts impulsive in dream
caught up in sub-brain episodes
sleep also performs out, outperforms language in
in so many ways? Rivers sleep. In cities I look
I enjoy beasts seen, sleep-writing leant dead
against window snow with my snooze hood up
while the cloud outsky asleep
communes in its sleep with my fast-boiling electric kettle
shapes thinking about Iceland loosely boiling
smally kettle sleep dreams of itself in me in a way
I wouldn't be focusing on more bleak if
I weren't capturing sleep word-by-word down
here nomen might see it ears perceive all sound
of the sleeps – that would be one reason unregistered
as I'm asleep it's all clearly snowy inside so there
state is in sleep intestate do you see any awake
being proffered? We want to go to sleep
right now we demand to be sleeping smiling
some part of the beneath-the-bed-writing
John Donne section stunk in sleep was yeah totally sleep-
like, not working because its pattern was
not fully realised here, or there acquiescent to hispast logics
his forebear slack-sleep self-organised
(organised soul and self) differently.

Imagine each lover's body
That it was *no* body, not thick dense
wax indie-shop record shelf-closed asleep to us
we each of us resists of each the other's work.
In my father the Lethean waters' sleeps
lap up him and sleeps soundly are his wet
ground getting relatively pooler per sleep
chain-sleep linking through us chosen, begot
or met, sideways sleep a bleaching snow seeks to melt
witnessed. Bygone, it was a gone-by scape
present in scope no sleep of as many eyes
burning their instruments as differential
sleep tones splitting on speech spitting each speech's fundamentals
Heart's sleeping thump, thumps sleeping, rests the steadier of hearts
to soundly sleep prone together hand in hand
Pax Vobiscum, a biscuit held jointly for time of snow
tomb-decoratively laid out, passed and coastal roads
waking we could be sounds stimulated upon

Contemporary Sad Dancers School

Belinda Carlisle has the same initials as B.C.
I'm interested for this project in why do people choose to dance out their sadness
why people make tracks sad, write them, sad ones
and their tracks are about sadness being danced out
and not just Belinda Carlisle's *Summer Rain* sadness or her tracks
also Suzanne Vega's
and whether Suzanne Vega is a vegetarian partly subconsciously because of her name.

Why Belinda Carlisle has the same initials as British Columbia.
Coincidentally *The Saddest Music In The World* is a Canadian film, set in Winnipeg, Manitoba.
Manitoba, co-coincidentally, is a very beautiful sad track by Edinburgh collective Mouth Music
but it'd be hard to dance to, fully, I think. I tried after I wrote that sentence and got lost in the beauty of it,
more sway than dance.

I'm interested in whether any of the members of Massive Attack will die from massive heart attacks
Unfinished Sympathy one of my favourite melancholy tracks to dance to.
I'm interested in whether the menu in *Tom's Diner* had any good vegetarian options
or just shit coffee from the 80s.
Soul II Soul have made me happy with two tracks spread apart in life time, mine
and could make me happy with more but I don't know them yet
Back to Life, *Keep on Movin'* and
Soul II Soul haven't got the same initials as anyone I can think of
– those Roman numerals –
not even Elizabeth II.
Yoko Ono releases dance tracks and she's nearly as old as the Queen.

But compilation, list, this thought track started by me wondering why we dance our sadnesses

and why it's almost a better feeling than dancing euphoric-wise.
Wise has me suddenly thinking of the straight-up pain wisdom of Eurythmics' *Somebody Told Me*,
After the event, dancing to our irredeemable failure to Moby's *Why does my heart feel so bad?*
can take us out of our horror, our bad, our loss-guilt, into a place where we make kindness to ourselves.
I've danced to a song about overcoming homophobia (*Small Town Boy*) and even performed its tortuous tessitura successfully live at karaoke.

Dancing sadly might make us less likely to pull and more likely to be loved.
Dancing sadly might make us less likely to pull or be pulled and more likely to love, to be loved
anonymously, in a letter, or an I SAW YOU column.
Madonna in her song *Heartbeat* from album Hard Candy
would rather not explain, it's just usual that the,
when she dances, she feels free, like the only one that the light shines on.

Our friends may know, as they dance with us, what's being released
and be our good friends in helping it out. Religiously.
Dancing is good exercise, since before the time of Christ,
is some sort of an exorcism if you
Keep on moving, don't stop, no, keep on moving
Keep on moving, keep on moving, don't stop, no
Keep on moving.
I hide myself from no one,
I hide myself from everyone.
I know the time will really come,
I know that no one will stay in my life, my life always,
whatever the colour of the sunrays
when you'll be in my life.

some notes

Drag Queen Poems were written in the autumn of 2015 after a summer in which I'd attended lots of drag events with my friend Wanda Isadora de Fourrure, aka the artist Jean-François Krebs. JL Williams instigated a plan to turn the poems into a performance, an idea which grew into '*The Library Is Open!*', a night of drag queen poetry at Scottish Poetry Library in January 2016. The Satoh referred to in number six is Japanese composer Somei Satoh (b. 1947) – check them out!

51'08" came out of a collaboration with Colin Herd for nick-e melville, Mirja Koponen and Gerry Smith's 2014 *Another Athens* project. The title refers to a timecode on a recording.

My Colonial Americana, Amerindian, North American, my Mork and Mindian poem was written for the event *One Night Without Us*, a spoken word celebration of the contribution of migrants to the UK held at The Fruitmarket Gallery, where I work, in February 2017.

Red Road and **miles come from Canada (to see this)** link to *Roads Read*, a collaboration with Leiza McLeod for Samantha Walton's 2015 Bath Spa University programme *Landscaping Change* which led to several different written and performance outcomes. These two poems come from a day waiting for, and missing, the demolition of Glasgow's Red Road flats.

'Is this what passes for conversion around here?' was written after attending in May 2009 at the General Assembly of the Church of Scotland, the counter-protest supporting the appointment as a minister of Scott Rennie, who was living openly in a same-sex relationship.

Little Requiem Mass uses words from the start of the different sections of the Latin Requiem Mass for the Dead, familiar as movement titles from the musical settings by Mozart, Verdi, Fauré and others. The English translations line up with the Latin in the poem margin.

The **Emily Dickinson Berlin sessions** are a sort of poem documentary of my time in Berlin in May 2015 at the *SoundOut!* festival. I was giving my performance *Subject Index*, in which I read out the complete poems of Emily Dickinson over a number of days dressed in a simulacrum of her famous white dress. I read in various public locations, including the Mehringdamm subway station. *it's mostly interruptions* mixes in lines from Dickinson's poems to notations of what was happening.

Censorable Poem maps itself onto the *Elegy for John Donne* by Joseph Brodsky which, as Auden noted in his introduction to the Penguin Modern European Poets edition that introduced it to English-reading audiences in 1973, uses the word 'sleep' 52 times. Colin Herd and I used the poem as a basis for a performance in London at the 2014 Camaradefest and Colin has a corresponding poem full of sleep too.

Rude Emily Dickinson. Believe it or not, this poem is made entirely of phrases from Emily Dickinson poems, taken out of context. I wrote down their, presumably accidental, smut to amuse myself as I worked through my marathon live readings of her work.

Contemporary Sad Dancers School was written for artist Alex Hetherington's anthology *Queer Information*. Alex, who also works under the alias Modern Edinburgh Film School, wanted to launch the anthology at a gay disco, and the poem was conceived as possible to perform with the playlist it mentions. There's a reading of it I did at Manchester's *The Other Room* series available to see online, where I cut the poem in and out of the named music tracks.

credits

Dragonflies in their surround was published online in Adjacent Pineapple issue 3 (2018). **Sunny Sutra** is recorded on the Scottish Poetry Library's podcast along with other poems and a discussion with JL Williams http://www.scottishpoetrylibrary.org.uk/connect/podcast/iain-morrison. **51'08"** was published by Freight in Gutter 15 (2016). **Glove Poems (in 5 fingers)** appeared on the centrefold pages of Zarf 5 (2016). Not one, but three versions of **gloss**, the first poem from **Emily Dickinson Berlin sessions**, were published by Modern Edinburgh Film School in a freesheet titled *Catherine Street - A Poetic Measurement, Modern Edinburgh Film School & a Reading Lecture, Iain Morrison* that was given away at the exhibition *Ripples On The Pond* at Glasgow's Gallery of Modern Art in June 2015. A version of **Censorable Poem** with added sheep and palindromes appeared in Glasgow's SPAM zine 3 (2016). **Contemporary Sad Dancers School** appeared in Modern Edinburgh Film School's *Queer Information* (2014) and also in The Other Room Anthology 9 (2017).

thanks

My hearty thanks to JL Williams and Jow Walton for reading this manuscript and providing encouragement, insight and killer cuts – if I have no other readers than yourselves, I will feel generously served. Thanks to my late father for having such pleasure in my work, and to my Mum who still reads it with indecipherable smiles. Thanks to Mark Reilly for a generous amount of cuddles per word. Thanks to the wonderful PiP group of Edinburgh's revolving cast of poets who have been my conversational, correspondent and intellectual companions over the last 7 years. To Sam Woods, for sustaining practical and long-term support. And of course thanks to Colin Waters. His instinct to choose me, his unbegrudging hard work, along with that of the whole Vagabond Voices team, and the sum of their kept faith have brought this book into your hands.